A CHILD'S TREASURE

Rosary Meditations For Children

Derek Rebello
Elsa Schiavone
Michael Boas
Illustrations by Maria Boas

Caritas Press, USA

A CHILD'S TREASURE
Rosary Meditations for Children

Derek Rebello, Elsa Schiavone, Michael Boas
Illustrations by Maria Boas

Edited by Sherry Boas
Copy edited by Rosie Schiavone

First Edition

10 9 8 7 6 5 4 3 2 1

ISBN 978 0-9833866-8-1

For reorders, visit LilyTrilogy.com or CatholicWord.com
Sherry@LilyTrilogy.com

Published by Caritas Press, Arizona, USA

For my Mom, who guides and inspires me.

---Elsa S.

For the souls of the unborn.

---Derek R.

For Monsignor Nestor, who inspires me to be a better altar server and more dedicated follower of Jesus.

---Michael B.

For Father Sergio, Father Juan and Father Doug, whose holy lives inspire me to become closer to Christ. And for my mother, who instilled in me a love for the Church.

---Maria B.

INTRODUCTION

Why should kids pray the rosary? Thinking about Jesus' life, death and resurrection helps to strengthen the bond between our souls and God.

St. Louis de Montfort said that praying the Rosary devoutly dons Jesus and Mary with crowns of red and white roses that never fade or whither. The word rosary means "crown of roses." Some people say they have even smelled the sweet aroma of roses while praying the rosary. Such is the power of these prayers to pierce the floor of heaven and allow a portion of paradise to seep through.

You can quiet your mind, heart and soul, breathing in the Holy Spirit, as you let the Rosary beads pass one by one through your fingers. Our Lady asks everyone to pray the Rosary every day to combat the evils of this world. We can change the future by praying the Rosary. It is a way for us to make the world a better place.

If we pray the Rosary faithfully and strive to live what we have learned, we will grow to love Jesus more, and loving Him means loving everyone God places in our lives. We will grow to love the Mass more because we will see unfolding at the altar all the things we have prayed through the Most Holy Rosary.

May your prayers bear great fruit in fostering in you an ever-growing devotion to Jesus, the Blessed Virgin Mary, and the Holy Mass.

THE
JOYFUL MYSTERIES

1.

THE ANNUNCIATION

"May it be done to me." Luke 1:38

When the angel Gabriel came to Mary to tell her she would have a son and He would be the savior, Mary must have had many questions and many fears. But knowing it was the will of God, she said, "Let it be done unto me according to your word." She answered yes to God.

Sometimes it is not easy doing what God wants us to do, but if it is God's will, we say yes, no matter what. Saying no to God can do nothing but make us sad

because it leads us away from God, who loves us and wants the best for us.

Sometimes it takes all our courage to say yes to God. In the times when it is difficult, we can ask God for help. We can pray for strength.

There are times in our life when we don't know what to do. We have to try to figure out God's will for us. We can pray and ask Him, and the answer will eventually come to us. We can ask our parents because we know they are wiser than we are, and God has given them to us to guide us in our life.

We do not always get to do what we want because sometimes the things we want are not the best for us. We might not always know what is best. But God does. Only God's will brings us true happiness. Look at the happiness that saying yes to God brought to Mary.

It's a great privilege to be the mother of a king, especially the king of the entire universe sent to save all of us and lead us to heaven. And Mary is now mother of us all. How joyful to have so many children to love! God has something wonderful in store for us too if we say yes to Him.

2.

THE VISITATION

"At the moment the sound of your greeting reached my ears, the infant in my womb leaped for joy." Luke 1:44

The Visitation is a moment of great joy. After the angel Gabriel told Mary that her cousin Elizabeth was going to have a baby, Mary set out on a journey to Elizabeth's house to offer her help. Filled with the Holy Spirit, Elizabeth realized Mary was carrying the Messiah in her womb. The baby in Elizabeth's womb, John the Baptist, leaped for joy because he, too, knew that God was near.

If we were like Elizabeth, we might live our lives differently. Elizabeth was able to recognize Jesus. Sometimes we don't. Even though we know every person is made in God's image, sometimes we fail to recognize Him in the people we really dislike or who are mean to us. Or in the homeless, the poor, the unemployed and the sick. Or when we do something that makes us feel really good, we sometimes fail to see that it was only by God's help that we did it. Sometimes at Mass, even though Jesus is there in the Eucharist, we are too busy thinking and complaining about our own cares and worries, and we don't give Him the respect He deserves.

Elizabeth, no doubt, felt comforted by Mary's arrival that day in the hills of Judea, knowing she would have help from her cousin. Mary was overjoyed because she knew she was doing the will of God by lightening her cousin's burden. Mary was always happy to do God's will. That is the only thing that brings us true joy - knowing we are doing what God wants.

Just as Elizabeth did, we can find comfort, too, in Mary's presence. She is our Mother, who comes to help us, watches over us and protects us from evil and lovingly guides us in all the things we must do every day. She especially helps us to love Jesus the way we should and to always try to do God's will so that we, too, will have true joy.

3.

THE NATIVITY

"You will find an infant wrapped in swaddling clothes and lying in a manger." Luke 2:12

Imagine how loving and innocent Jesus must have looked as a newborn baby, lying in a bed of hay in a feeding trough for animals. When we imagine His adorable face, we think about how much God loves us, that He sent us His son so that we could be saved. When we imagine looking into baby Jesus' eyes, His spirit suddenly flows within us, and we realize that He loves us. Maybe our hearts beat a little faster for the love of Jesus. If we could be like one of the shepherds that night, we would be in such awe. To come to that humble stable and find the

King of Heaven and Earth! They had great joy, for they had just seen the proof of their salvation. When we imagine touching His tiny hand, we feel as if we are already in heaven. But not without a huge price. All the pieces of straw that we see in His manger, remind us of all the big things He would have to suffer to save our souls.

When we look at Joseph and Mary, we can think about our own parents and how hard they try to imitate these perfect examples that Jesus' parents were. We remember how Mary always said yes to God and always wanted to do His will, and that is why we have Jesus. And when we think of Joseph, we think of how hard he worked to find the perfect place for Mary to have her baby and how he worked so hard as a carpenter to provide for them and how much he loved his little family.

And now, we ask ourselves what we must do to love Jesus as we should. Joseph and Mary must have been overjoyed and honored that they were trusted and chosen for such a privilege. God has great plans for us too. If we obey, listen and pray, we will discover what God wants for us, and inside His will, we will find our joy.

4.

THE PRESENTATION

"They took him up to Jerusalem to present him to the Lord."

Luke 2:22

In the Temple, there was a Prophet named Simeon, who had been promised by God that he would one day see the Messiah. Simeon was growing very old and had waited a long time, but he never gave up hope.

When Joseph and Mary brought Jesus into the Temple, the Holy Spirit revealed to

Simeon that Jesus was the one that he and all the Jewish people had been waiting for. He was the Savior of the world. When Simeon took Jesus in his arms, he was so happy. He knew his life was complete. He had waited such a long time, but God kept His promise, as He always does.

Maybe Simeon recognized Jesus because he was always looking for Him. He might have looked for Him all his life, knowing that God would not let him down. What if we had our eyes always open to seeing Jesus? Where would we see Him? Would we see Him in our "Temple" - in Church? Would we see him "hiding" in the bread, consecrated by the priest and changed into the body of Christ?

Simeon was watchful, waiting and patient, and he was rewarded with the opportunity to hold the savior of the world in his arms. What if we could hold this precious baby in our arms? How would it change us?

When we receive Communion, we are holding Jesus inside ourselves. We are even closer to Him than if we were holding Him in our arms.

5.

FINDING JESUS IN THE TEMPLE

"When his parents saw him, they were astonished, and his mother said to him, "Son, why have you done this to us? Your father and I have been looking for you with great anxiety." And he said to them, "Why were you looking for me? Did you not know that I must be in my Father's House?" Luke 2:48-49

It must have been horrible for Mary and Joseph when they could not find Jesus. They must have felt desperate and in terrible anguish to think they might never see Him again.

Sometimes it feels like we are desperately searching for Jesus too. When we feel sad, when we are trying to make a decision about what is right or wrong, we know that He will help us. We just need to keep searching

until we find Him. When we find God's will for us, we will find Jesus. And then, we too, will have great joy like Joseph and Mary did when they found their son.

How do we know God's will for us? God has given us gifts to guide us to His will: our parents, our prayers and our Church.

It says in Scripture that, after being found in the Temple, Jesus went home with Mary and Joseph and was obedient to His parents. Why would Jesus, who is God, King of the Universe, have to be obedient to anyone?

It's not always easy to be obedient. It takes a lot of effort and humility. But Jesus Himself showed us by example the importance of being obedient to parents. The Lord values our obedience to our parents so much that He made it one of the Ten Commandments. God put our parents here to teach us about Him and to teach us what is right so that we might also be obedient to God and the Holy Catholic Church, as well as our parents.

The good habits we form as children will most likely stay with us all our lives. If we are obedient to our parents as children, it will be easier for us to obey God when we are adults, and we will always have the joy the Holy Family had in knowing we are doing God's will.

THE LUMINOUS MYSTERIES

1.

THE BAPTISM OF JESUS

"After Jesus was baptized, he came up from the water and behold, the heavens were opened for him, and he saw the Spirit of God descending like a dove and coming upon him."

Matthew 3:16

John the Baptist must have been surprised that Jesus, who was the Messiah, would want to be baptized by him. He probably did not feel worthy for such an honor. Jesus, of course, had no sin, so He was not in need of Baptism. But He wanted to set an example for us to follow. If He, who is God, is humble enough to be baptized, why shouldn't we, who are sinful, do the same?

Baptism is a sign that we are God's children and that He loves us. The Sacrament of Baptism is like God welcoming you into his family and setting you aside for a special purpose that no one else can do but you. Your Baptism day is really like the day of your birth, when you are born into the Kingdom of God.

Our parents have us baptized because they want us to know, love and serve God and receive all the graces given through the sacraments, which are like rungs on a ladder leading to Jesus. Our parents want us to become children of God and receive all of God's blessings. May we always be grateful to God for this amazing gift of Faith and to our parents for passing it on to us.

2.

THE WEDDING FEAST AT CANA

"When the wine ran short, the mother of Jesus said to him, 'They have no wine.' And Jesus said to her, 'Woman, how does your concern affect me? My hour has not yet come.' His mother said to the servers, 'Do whatever he tells you.'"

John 2:3-5

Mary told Jesus that the wedding host had run out of wine because she knew her son could do amazing things. She felt sorry for the bride and groom and the host of the wedding. She knew they would be embarrassed over not having enough wine for their guests. She had faith that Jesus would do whatever was necessary to bring about something good from the problem. Mary told the wine servers "do whatever He tells you," because she knows only good can come from doing as Jesus says.

Turning water into wine at the wedding feast is Jesus' first miracle. It tells us something very important about Mary.

Just as she pointed out to Jesus the needs of the wedding host when the wine was gone, she'll also point out our needs to Jesus when we ask her to intercede for us. We know that Mother Mary will take all our prayers to Jesus because she cares for us and she loves us. We ask Mother Mary to intercede for us because she is much holier than we are and Jesus loves her so much that it is hard for Him to refuse her.

Throughout her life, Mary was always a perfect example of faith and trust in Jesus. We should try to imitate her in every way, at every chance we get.

3.

THE PROCLAMATION OF THE KINGDOM

"After John had been arrested, Jesus came to Galilee proclaiming the gospel of God: 'This is the time of fulfillment. The kingdom of God is at hand. Repent, and believe in the gospel.'"

Mark 1:14-15

Jesus told His disciples to let the children come to Him, because the kingdom of God belongs to children.

Maybe that is because children are more humble, and it is easier for them to accept Jesus' words. They are less likely to sin and are more innocent and holy. They are not afraid to ask questions. And because children are not proud, it is easier for them to forgive.

We can imagine how joyful and blessed we would have felt sitting at Jesus' feet, listening to Him tell us about the Kingdom of God and how we can one day go there. Every time we go to church, we have that same opportunity. To have Jesus come into our midst through the Holy Eucharist and to hear the word of God proclaimed to us through Holy Scripture.

In the Holy Mass, Jesus speaks to us through the priest. In reading the Holy Bible, we can learn about how much Jesus loves us and how much he wants us to be with Him in heaven one day.

He often talks to us, yet we are too busy with our own cares and worries to take a moment to listen to Him. When we sit quietly before the Blessed Sacrament in adoration, it is easier for us to hear Him. Through prayers, such as the Rosary, He can tell us about His life, death and resurrection.

4.

THE TRANSFIGURATION

"Jesus took with him Peter, James, and John … and led them up a high mountain by themselves. And he was transfigured before them; his face shone like the sun and his clothes became white as light … behold, a bright cloud cast a shadow over them, then from the cloud came a voice that said, "This is my beloved Son, with whom I am well pleased; listen to him." When the disciples heard this, they fell prostrate and were very much afraid. But Jesus came and touched them, saying, "Rise, and do not be afraid."

Matthew 17:1-7

It was as if Peter, James and John were getting a glimpse of Heaven when they saw Jesus, shining like the sun, and the prophets of old standing beside Him. At that moment, it was like heaven touched earth. When we go to Mass, we can get a glimpse of heaven too. When the priest is consecrating the bread and wine, it is like heaven on earth. The priest acts for Jesus and the bread and wine becomes Jesus, so we are actually with Jesus whenever we go to church. And wherever Jesus is, that is Heaven to us.

Maybe through the Transfiguration, God was also trying to tell the apostles that Jesus is the fulfillment of the Old Testament, that He is the Messiah the prophets had spoken about.

Maybe Jesus allowed the three apostles this vision to reassure them that He was truly the Son of God because He knew that He was going to die soon and the apostles needed hope, comfort, strength and courage. Through prayer and the sacraments, He offers us these same gifts even today, for all the crosses we have to bear.

Peter, James and John were probably amazed that God chose them to see such a sight as the Transfiguration of Jesus. They were the only ones who got this glimpse into heaven. It was a great privilege to be chosen. When we go to Mass, we are privileged as they were, because we get a glimpse into heaven too.

5.

THE INSTITUTION OF THE HOLY EUCHARIST

"Jesus took bread, said the blessing, broke it and giving it to his disciples, said, 'Take and eat. This is my body.' Then he took a cup, gave thanks and gave it to them, saying, 'drink from it, all of you, for this is my blood of the Covenant, which will be shed on behalf of many for the forgiveness of sins.'"

Matthew 26:26-27

Imagine if we could have been there at the Last Supper, the first Mass. We would have not been able to believe that we were chosen to partake in this incredible mystery

of receiving Christ into ourselves. And yet, that's the way it is for us at every Mass. Even two thousand years later, it is as if we are at the first Mass every time the priest consecrates the body and blood of Christ. It is like time has been erased and we have traveled back in time to that first Mass. The Eucharist is Jesus' love for us passed down throughout the ages. Receiving Communion is heaven meeting earth, the Son of God coming into our hearts. The Eucharist means the world to us who receive it because we become one with Christ. When we receive the Eucharist, at that moment, we become what we eat - the body of Christ. The word Communion means "together, in unison, as one." What an incredible blessing to be one with Christ who loves us so much. Being one with Him, we want to avoid sin because we love Jesus and we don't want to hurt Him. We know He wants to be in a clean and pure place, a loving place, not in a sinful body. We long to give Jesus love in return for the love He gives us.

Jesus loves us so much, He wanted to stay with us always, so He gives Himself to us as bread. Jesus never leaves us. He will never stop loving us.

THE SORROWFUL MYSTERIES

1.

AGONY IN THE GARDEN

"Not my will, but yours be done." Luke 22:42

When they came to arrest Jesus in the garden, Peter drew his sword to protect Jesus, but our Lord did not want anyone to get hurt. In fact, He healed the injury that Peter inflicted on a servant of those coming to arrest Him. We know, from our own lives, how difficult this must have been for Jesus to give only love in return for all the horrible things people were doing to Him. We get so upset over much, much smaller things. When people take advantage of us, it's hard to pray for them, even though that is what God wants us to do. Or when it seems that someone is not really listening to what we are saying or not trying to understand us, it's hard to be patient and explain what we really mean. Or when people brag and boast about what they can do or what they have, it's difficult to swallow our pride and not boast or brag about ourselves or put them down. It's hard to avoid being prideful and snap at people when they say something rude. But we have to try to treat others with love no matter what, because that's what God wants us to do.

Jesus always strived to do what God the Father wanted Him to do, even when it was extremely hard. Jesus knew all along He would have to suffer. He knew that God had planned for Him to die to save the world. In the garden of Gethsemane, Jesus prayed to God the Father, "Your will be done, not mine." This helps us understand how much Jesus trusted God the Father and how much He loves us, that He even died for us.

As children, we need to look for God's will inside our parent's will for us. We have to do what our parents want us to do, so that we can please God. He wants us to listen to our parents because God gave parents the wisdom to teach their children about life and how to do things that please God. We must always try to follow the example of Jesus, who tried to please His earthly parents, Mary and Joseph, as well as His Father in heaven. Jesus' words to His heavenly Father, "not my will, but yours be done" are an inspiration to us. We can use them in our prayers and try to remember them at every moment, especially when Jesus is asking something difficult of us.

2.

THE SCOURGING AT THE PILLAR

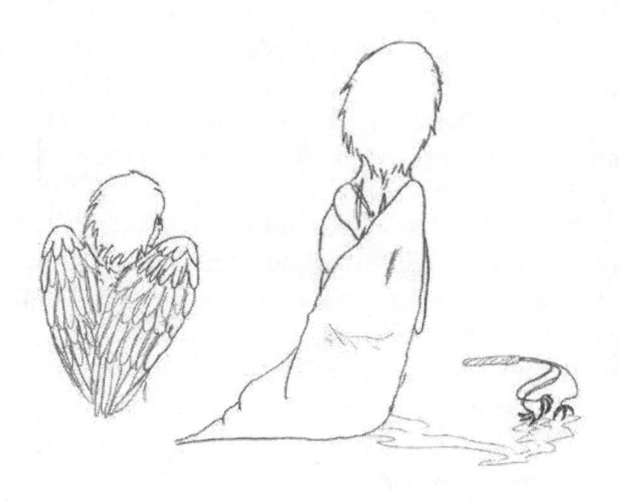

"By His stripes we were healed."
Isaiah 53:5

The scourging was so cruel and inhumane, and in addition to the horrible physical pain, the scourging must have hurt Jesus even more because He did not deserve it. He went through the pain purely out of love because, without it, none of us would ever go to heaven.

Sometimes we get blamed for something that isn't completely our fault, and we get upset right away. We don't think of how Jesus quietly and willingly suffered some-

thing much, much worse even though He didn't deserve it. He forgave those who tortured Him and asked His Father to forgive them too.

The Bible refers to His wounds as His "stripes." And it says that by those stripes we are healed. Because Jesus suffered for us, we are forgiven for our sins and are able to go to heaven. We might be healed from the sin of pride, including jealousy, bragging, dishonesty, arrogance, vanity, conceit and selfishness; the sin of impatience, which can lead to the inability to control our anger; the sins of gossiping, criticizing, rudeness, hatred, laziness and despair or hopelessness.

All of the thrashes from the whips are the hundreds of thousands of sins we commit, being thrashed away, blow by blow. When we think of the scourging, we feel sad about how many sins we've committed, all the pain Jesus had to bear for our sake. It makes us want to run to confession. It makes us feel sorry for Jesus and want to serve Him more. There are many ways we can serve Him, including going to Mass and being attentive to all the readings, songs and prayers, and loving all the people God has put in our lives.

3.

THE CROWNING WITH THORNS

"Weaving a crown of thorns, they placed it on his head and a reed in his right hand. And kneeling before him, they mocked him, saying, 'Hail, King of the Jews!' They spat upon him..."

Matthew 27:29-30

The Roman soldiers mocked Jesus by calling Him the king of the Jews and putting a crown of thorns on Him. It was excruciating to have sharp thorns piercing into His head, but our Lord must have been thinking about who He was suffering for and who would benefit from the thorns. All the thorns on His crown are all of our sins He needed to bear, an extra weight while carrying the cross.

It's amazing how kind Jesus was, even while He was suffering. If someone else hurts us, it's easy to get upset at that person, even if

we know it's an accident. And if the pain isn't even caused by another person, it often makes us angry, even though there is no one to be angry at. But Jesus never got angry with those who were hurting Him. Instead of hating, Jesus chose to love and forgive, and instead of feeling sorry for Himself, He told the women of Jerusalem to weep for themselves and their children and not for Him.

When we are mocked or made fun of like Jesus was, it makes us feel hurt and sad. We can try to ignore it or we can try to laugh along with those who are mocking us. But neither of those options seem to take away the hurt feelings. If we remember that our Lord was mocked as well, we can unite our hurt feelings with His and we too can try to forgive instead of hate.

Forgiving is not always an easy thing to do. Sometimes, it's actually painful not to seek revenge. We want to lash out in anger. But those are the times we should think about Jesus' burdens and shouldn't place yet another thorn on His sacred head by committing another sin.

Instead of a crown of thorns, Jesus should have worn a King's crown, golden and full of light. Yet, for a brief time in history, He had to suffer the thorns. The splendid crown is, for sure, His now. And yet, when we picture Jesus, we might not picture Him with a crown at all, even though we know He is King of heaven and earth. Maybe we more often picture Him with his arms open and smiling, ready to love and forgive us, just as He loved and forgave those who hurt Him so badly.

4.

THE CARRYING OF THE CROSS

"As they were going out, they met a Cyrenian named Simon; this man they pressed into service to carry the cross."

Matthew 27:32

Jesus probably felt very sad while carrying the cross, thinking about what the children of God were doing to Him. Many of the onlookers just stared and did nothing. Some of them even added to His suffering by ridiculing Him, jeering at Him, throwing things at Him, and still Jesus showed nothing but love and mercy.

Jesus was probably thinking about us, about how we would act in our lives. He hoped we would be good children of God and not flee

from Him like the lost sheep. Jesus knows all and could have told the future and seen the things we would do that would make Him suffer greatly. Every single splinter in the wood of the cross is one of our sins pressing on Him. We can take that burden away by going to confession and deciding, with all our heart, never to sin again.

It is shocking that anyone would do such horrible things to Jesus, and we would be grateful if we could help Jesus in the smallest way, if we could help Him carry the cross like Simon of Cyrene. We can help Him carry His cross by carrying ours willingly, without complaining. We can give up little things that are bad for us. We can say something kind to someone who is rude to us or say a prayer for that person instead of thinking bad things about him or her.

It's a wonder that, although He is God and all powerful, Jesus allowed Himself to be weak and fall under the weight of the cross. Maybe He was trying to show us what humility is. Maybe He allowed it because He knew it would soften hearts. Everything He did was to purify hearts and lead souls to heaven. We can let Jesus purify our hearts by staying close to Him as He suffers on the way to Calvary. In our lives, that means always remembering the price Jesus paid for our salvation and trying as hard as we can not to sin again.

5.

THE CRUCIFIXION

"The earth quaked, rocks were split, tombs were opened and the bodies of many saints who had fallen asleep were raised."

Matthew 27:51-52

Of all the apostles, John was the only one who stayed with Jesus at the foot of the cross, comforting his mother, Mary, who was so heartbroken and horrified over the torture being inflicted on her son. Mary and John were experiencing so much sadness themselves and probably feeling very fearful and powerless, yet they stayed with Jesus and kept Him company every step of

the way so that Jesus would not be alone in His suffering. Even though it was hard not to run away, they did not abandon Jesus. We, too, love Jesus and Mary so much that we would want to be there for them in their time of greatest need and sorrow. Hopefully our fears would not have gotten in the way of our love for them. And hopefully, in our daily lives, love will also win out over fear, especially in the times when it is hard to stand by Jesus. Sometimes we try to share our faith with others and they just don't understand, or they might even get upset with us. Sometimes we might be called to participate in peaceful protests to defend our freedom of religion. It might be uncomfortable or inconvenient, but we do it out of love.

Love is what allowed Mary to endure what was happening to her son as she stood at the foot of the cross. She accepted God's will because she knew the crucifixion was necessary for the forgiveness of sins. We are her sons and daughters too, and she wanted all of us to be saved, and that was the work her son was accomplishing on the cross. If the crucifixion had never happened, no one could go to heaven because we are all sinners and none of us deserve eternal life. Yet Jesus is so loving and merciful that He died for us so we can be happy forever in heaven.

THE GLORIOUS MYSTERIES

1.

THE RESURRECTION

"Do not let your hearts be troubled ... In my father's house there are many dwelling places. If there were not, would I have told you that I am going to prepare a place for you? And if I go and prepare a place for you, I will come back again and take you to myself, so that where I am you also may be."

John 14: 1-3

We can imagine what it was like for Mary Magdalene to find Jesus alive in the garden outside the tomb. Maybe we would be speechless at the sight of His great glory, His kind face, His gentle hands, still with the nail marks that won our salvation.

The Resurrection is a great triumph that we can hold in our hearts as a reason to always have hope! When Jesus came back from the dead after suffering that horrible death on the cross, God proved that Light is stronger than darkness. Life is stronger than death. Love is more powerful than sin. Only truth can win. Jesus is the truth, the way and the life.

This gives us great hope. At the end of our lives, we too will be resurrected. God raises us up from the dead and brings us to a new home, new life and a happy eternity in heaven.

If we always keep this thought with us as we go through life, nothing will cause us to lose our hope. If we always seek to please Him, not even our worst day can take away what God has ready for us in heaven. We no longer need to fear anything. Eternal happiness will be ours if we persevere in doing His will in our lives.

2.

THE ASCENSION

"As he blessed them, he parted from them and was taken up to heaven."

Luke 24:51

After all the suffering He went through, the day came when Jesus could finally go see His Father again. It must have been hard, in a way, for His disciples to see Him leave, but He told them He would go prepare a place for them, so that they could one day join Him in heaven. We too will join Him someday, and we will get to spend

eternity with Jesus and Mary and all the angels and saints and our loved ones who have died. It will be a place where there is only light, and no hint of darkness, not even our shadows. There's no sickness, no pain, no sadness. Just the pure joy of being with God and those we love.

Until then, we can possess a bit of heaven right here on earth. Jesus loves us so much, He didn't want to just stay with us for the thirty-three years He was living His earthly life. He wanted to stay with us forever. And so, He told His disciple before His ascension, "behold, I am with you always, even until the end of the age." He remains with us forever, body and soul, in the Holy Eucharist, and He is with us in spirit everywhere we go.

It helps to remember, especially on hard days, that even though Jesus ascended into heaven, He is still with us, and we can always talk to Him. Whether we are saying the rosary or participating in the Mass, or just saying a simple prayer in the middle of our day. Jesus will be with us forever, whether we are in Heaven or on Earth.

3.

THE DESCENT OF THE HOLY SPIRIT

"If you love me, you will keep my commandments. And I will ask the Father, and He will give you another advocate to be with you always, the Spirit of truth, which the world cannot accept, because it neither sees nor knows it. But you know it, because it remains with you, and will be in you. I will not leave you orphans; I will come to you."

John 14:15-17

The Holy Spirit is a light in dark places. We need this light to guide us to God, just as a lantern lights our path through the dark woods. We need the light of the Holy Spirit to defeat the darkness that tries to consume us when we sin by doing things that are displeasing to God, such as making fun of someone or failing to pay attention at Mass.

The Holy Spirit is especially powerful at Mass. He comes down on the bread and wine and turns them into the body and blood of Christ. When we receive the Eucharist, we are receiving the Light into our bodies and souls, which become radiant, joyful, happy, beautiful and full of God Himself.

The Holy Spirit offers many gifts: Wisdom, Understanding, Counsel, Fortitude, Knowledge, Piety and Fear of the Lord. We can ask the Lord for these gifts when we wake up every morning. That will help us make good decisions and have a day that is pleasing to God.

Whenever we are inspired to do something good, it is the Holy Spirit working in our lives. That's why whenever we do something that makes us feel good about ourselves, we should thank Him.

4.

THE ASSUMPTION

"Therefore my heart is glad and my soul rejoices, my body, too, abides in confidence; Because you will not abandon my soul to the nether world, nor will you suffer your faithful one to undergo corruption."

Psalms 16:9-10

When Mary's earthly life was over, she was taken, body and soul, into heaven. Jesus took Mary to heaven, body and soul, because she is the heavenly queen and Jesus is the heavenly king, and the two have to be together.

Mary received this special privilege because, all of her life, she never said no to God. She loved Jesus more than anyone else. She never sinned and she always accepted God's will.

Mary's body is special because she was the first tabernacle. Her womb was the first place Jesus dwelled on earth. Even before the manger, He was living within her. Because Mary carried Jesus in her womb, body and soul, Jesus carried Mary, body and soul, into heaven.

Though the end of our earthly life will be different from Mary's, she is for us a sign of great hope, because we are also made for heaven, created to be great saints, made to be happy with God forever. May we always strive to love Jesus and try to please God the way Mary did so we can someday join her with all the saints in heaven.

5.

THE CORONATION

"A great sign appeared in the sky, a woman clothed with the sun, with the moon under her feet, and on her head a crown of twelve stars." Revelation 12:1

During her earthly life, Mary was poor, humble and unknown. She never sought honor or riches. No matter how many graces God bestowed on her, she never considered herself better than anyone else. She wished to remain quiet and humble, always waiting to hear what God had planned for her. Because of this, Jesus thought she was so special, He gave her the most beautiful crown and the highest honor in heaven.

Her crown must be indescribable in its gilded golden glory. We don't know what it looks like, but maybe it has red jewels for her Son's precious blood that saved souls and white diamonds for the water that poured from His side and washes souls clean.

It must have been an amazing day in heaven on the day Mary was crowned, a brilliant light shining forth from her, with all the angels and saints gathered around, admiring her for her virtues. Still that day, she maintained her humility, even though she became the queen of heaven.

We too should strive to be humble like Mary, always listening for God's voice, always trying to seek His will. If we do, we can be sure, God has something wonderful in store for us too.

HOW TO PRAY THE ROSARY

1. While holding the crucifix, make the SIGN OF THE CROSS: "In the name of the Father, and of the Son and of the Holy Spirit. Amen."

2. Then, recite the APOSTLE'S CREED:
"I BELIEVE IN GOD, the Father almighty, Creator of heaven and earth, and in Jesus Christ, his only Son, our Lord, who was conceived by the Holy Spirit, born of the Virgin Mary, suffered under Pontius Pilate, was crucified, died and was buried; he descended into hell; on the third day he rose again from the dead; he ascended into heaven, and is seated at the right hand of God the Father almighty; from there he will come to judge the living and the dead. I believe in the Holy Spirit, the holy catholic Church, the communion of saints, the forgiveness of sins, the resurrection of the body, and life everlasting. Amen."

3. Recite the OUR FATHER on the first large Bead:
"OUR FATHER, Who art in heaven, Hallowed be Thy Name. Thy Kingdom come. Thy Will be done, on earth as it is in Heaven. Give us this day our daily bread. And forgive us our trespasses, as we forgive

those who trespass against us. And lead us not into temptation, but deliver us from evil. Amen."

4. On each of the three small beads, recite a HAIL MARY for the increase of faith, hope and love. "HAIL MARY, full of grace, the Lord is with thee; Blessed art thou among women, and blessed is the fruit of thy womb, Jesus. Holy Mary, Mother of God, pray for us sinners, now and at the hour of death. Amen."

5. Recite the GLORY BE on the next large bead.
"GLORY BE to the Father, and to the Son, and to the Holy Spirit. As it was in the beginning, is now, and ever shall be, world without end. Amen."

6. Recall the first Rosary Mystery and recite the Our Father on the next large bead.

7. On each of the adjacent ten small beads (known as a decade), recite a Hail Mary while reflecting on the mystery.

8. On the next large bead, recite the Glory Be.

9. The FATIMA PRAYER may be said here:

"O MY JESUS, forgive us our sins, save us from the fires of hell, lead all souls to heaven, especially those who are in most need of Thy mercy."

10. Begin the next decade by recalling the next mystery and reciting an Our Father. Move to the small beads and pray 10 Hail Marys while meditating on the mystery.

11. Continue until you have circled the entire Rosary (five decades.) Or for a full Rosary, you will circle it four times (twenty decades.)

12. It is customary to CONCLUDE with the following prayers:

HAIL HOLY QUEEN

"HAIL, HOLY QUEEN, mother of mercy, our life, our sweetness, and our hope. To thee do we cry, poor banished children of Eve. To thee do we send up our sighs, mourning and weeping in this valley of tears. Turn then, most gracious advocate, thine eyes of mercy toward us, and after this our exile, show us the blessed fruit of thy womb, Jesus. O clement, O loving, O sweet Virgin Mary.
(Verse) Pray for us, O Holy Mother of God.

(Response) That we may be made worthy of the promises of Christ."

ROSARY PRAYER

(Verse) Let us pray,
(Response) O God, whose only begotten Son, by His life, death, and resurrection, has purchased for us the rewards of eternal salvation, grant, we beseech Thee, that while meditating on these mysteries of the most holy Rosary of the Blessed Virgin Mary, that we may both imitate what they contain and obtain what they promise, through Christ our Lord. Amen.

Most Sacred Heart of Jesus, have mercy on us.

Immaculate Heart of Mary, pray for us.

In the Name of the Father, and of the Son and of the Holy Spirit. Amen.

FICTION AVAILABLE FROM
Caritas Press / Catholic Word

Until Lily

Wherever Lily Goes

Life Entwined with Lily's

Sherry Boas' life-changing series that has been called: **"masterful," "profound," "riveting," "heart-wrenching"** and **"made for our times."**

Coming Spring 2013
The Things Lily Knew

A brilliant Rhodes Scholar whose love life is torn in threes, Annabel Greeley is not lacking in wit or intellect. But when the accomplished geneticist is faced with a decision that will change, not only her life, but the future of humanity, the answers elude her. She is hounded by the ever-present and unavoidable fact that she would not be alive if it weren't for her Aunt Lily, who happened to have Down syndrome and, seemingly, all of life's answers. Annabel's life is about to change in profound and paradoxical ways as she sets out in search of the things Lily knew.

Visit www.LilyTrilogy.com

www.LilyTrilogy.com

Caritas Press

(602) 920-2846

Sherry@LilyTrilogy.com

Made in the USA
San Bernardino, CA
09 March 2014